THE GREAT PACIFIC AIR OFFENSIVE OF WORLD WAR II

Volume 2

Severing the Empire's Lifeline 1945

John W. Lambert

Schiffer Military History
Atglen, PA

Dustjacket artwork by Steve Ferguson, Colorado Springs, CO.

RICKENBACKER TO BONG
Depicted here is the fighter sweep by 5th AF P-38 Lightnings over the Japanese 4th Air Army HQ at Hollandia, New Guinea, on 12 April 1944. Attached to Maj. Jay Robbin's 80th Squadron "HEADHUNTERS" for the mission was leading ace Maj. Dick Bong. The major was the last surviving twenty-victory ace in the deadly race to break the World War I record set by Eddie Rickenbacker, and there after tied in December of 1942 by USMC Capt. Joe Foss. In February 1944, USMC Capt. Bob Hanson set the new mark at twenty-five, only to be killed by enemy ground fire a few days thereafter. On 3 March, Bong's widely publicized P-38 "MARGE" had carried him up to the Rickenbacker-Foss aerial victory mark of twenty-four confirmed, but MARGE was lost just days later by another pilot. The replacement Lightning "2104380" in its red trim was quickly drawn from the 5 FC HQ reserves, and as illustrated here, its displays a rectangular discoloration forward of the scoreboard where MARGE's portrait would have been added. However, the Hollandia raids made the portrait much less of an issue, and on 3 April, the ace tied the "Hanson mark" of twenty-five. Nine days later, out of the nine enemy fighters confirmed that day, Bong gunned down a trio of Ki-43 OSCARs to bring his score up to twenty-eight. With that last victim, Bong secured the lead over all the U.S. services worldwide. Six months later in the Philippines campaign, Dick Bong would be cited with the Congressional Medal of Honor for thirty-six victories, just as legends Rickenbacker, Foss and Hanson had previously been honored. His tour ended in late December with his fortieth victory; the record that stands to this day.

Acknowledgments
We are indebted to the following individuals and organizations for assistance in providing photos and information: Jim Crow, Ken Daniels, Wally Forman, Leon Frankel, Bill Hess, Fred Johnsen, Bob Livingstone, Ernie McDowell, Jerry Scutts, Richard Simms, Roy Snapp, Don Sweet, Barrett Tillman, Bill Wolf, U.S. National Archives (NARS), Washington, DC; the Museum of Naval Aviation (MNA), Pensacola, Florida; Air Force Museum, Wright-Patterson, Ohio, U.S. Air Force (USAF); U.S. Navy (USN); and the U.S. Marine Corps (USMC).

Book design by John W. Lambert.
Cover design by Robert Biondi.

Copyright © 2005 by John W. Lambert.
Library of Congress Catalog Number: 2005924764.

Printed in China.
ISBN: 0-7643-2267-2

We are always looking for people to write books on new and related subjects. If you have an idea for a book, please contact us at the address below.

Published by Schiffer Publishing Ltd.
4880 Lower Valley Road
Atglen, PA 19310
Phone: (610) 593-1777
FAX: (610) 593-2002
E-mail: Info@schifferbooks.com.
Visit our web site at: www.schifferbooks.com
Please write for a free catalog.
This book may be purchased from the publisher.
Please include $3.95 postage.
Try your bookstore first.

In Europe, Schiffer books are distributed by:
Bushwood Books
6 Marksbury Ave.
Kew Gardens
Surrey TW9 4JF
England
Phone: 44 (0)20 8392-8585
FAX: 44 (0)20 8392-9876
E-mail: Bushwd@aol.com.
Free postage in the UK. Europe: air mail at cost.
Try your bookstore first.

FOREWORD

World War II in the Pacific began with an attack by Japanese aircraft carrier units against Oahu on 7 December 1941. From that time until the conclusion of hostilities in August 1945 the conflict was dominated by air power strategy for both the Allies and the Japanese. In the final analysis Allied air power proved decisive in achieving victory

There were no land masses in the broad reaches of the Pacific Ocean where great armies could clash, unlike the struggles in North Africa, Eastern Europe or the Western Front. The battles in the adjacent China-Burma-India theater of operations were the sole exception.

By mid 1942 the post Pearl Harbor Japanese juggernaut had reached to Australia and Southeast Asia. The Allies finally held the line, during the aircraft carrier conflicts in the Coral Sea and at Midway and with desperate ground actions in New Guinea and the Solomons Islands, and by 1943 the Japanese were forced on the defensive.

This volume depicts the Allied offensive drive that followed. In this vast region there were no islands where more than a handful of infantry divisions would meet in face-to-face struggles, New Guinea, the Philippines, and Okinawa being the most notable exceptions. In these and other islands ground forces engaged in bitter fighting in appalling terrain under dreadful conditions. But the strategic plan of General Douglas MacArthur and Admiral Chester Nimitz was not to seize territory but airfields or ground that would lend itself to the construction of airfields. They were viewed as the strategic stepping stones to Japan. Aviation engineers often worked under fire to hew new air bases out of jungle, coral, or volcanic rock. With each new airfield complex the range of Allied land-based aircraft was advanced, permitting new areas of Japanese territory to come under air attack.

Even the titanic naval battles of the Pacific were primarily contests between carrier-based forces. Only in a handful of encounters did large fleets of warships engage each other in brief surface gun battles.

In virtually every Pacific campaign, the Allied air forces sought to achieve aerial supremacy, interdict Japanese maritime supply lines, and isolate the battlefield. When this was accomplished enemy ground forces were either destroyed by air power or bypassed. Some Japanese-held islands were never invaded and their garrisons never engaged. They could neither attack nor retreat because of the supremacy of Allied air power Thus they were left to wither in the wake of the advance. With hindsight it became apparent that Allied air power had become so dominant that some islands were invaded needlessly.

The targets of both carrier-based and land-based Allied air forces were largely tactical until the island-hopping strategy allowed B-29 Superforts to begin the final strategic aerial campaign against Japanese home island-industry in late 1944.

Along the path of the Pacific Allied advance air battles never achieved numbers approaching the thousand-plane strategic air raids that were launched from England. Still the air campaigns for domination of the Solomons and New Guinea were fought until the virtual destruction of one air force or the other. Likewise carrier vs. carrier battles generally saw the near annihilation of the losers air groups.

By late 1942 both Japanese and U.S. Navy aircraft carrier units had been dramatically reduced by the early contests: Coral Sea, Midway, Santa Cruz. The Japanese, however, had few carrier replacements while United States shipbuilding capacity began to spawn dozens of new carriers that would scourge the central Pacific with near impunity.

In 1943 the Allies seized the initiative from the Japanese in the Southwest Pacific with victories in New Guinea and the Solomons and began the offensive drive that would breach Japan's Pacific defense ring in the Carolines.

Subsequent carrier battles, such as the First Battle of the Philippine Sea, found hundreds of aircraft engaged on both sides. The Allied approach to the Philippines was a magnet for Japanese reserve squadrons from Formosa, China and the home islands. It was here that the desperate Japanese began to employ Kamikaze tactics.

By the end of 1944 Allied air power had advanced the bomb line to the Japanese homeland, with new c arrier task forces, a continuous string of new island air bases, and new and improved aircraft. Once the air offensive reached Japan hundreds of aircraft clashed in the skies over Kyushu and Honshu.

This is a pictorial history of those intrepid airmen and the aircraft that battled for control of the Pacific Ocean during the great Allied air offensive of World War II..

These photos have been obtained from the private collections of veterans and from various official archives, all noted in "Acknowledgments." Some archival views may have been previously published, since they are in the public domain. Information accompanying official photos was frequently cryptic, incomplete, or incorrect. However, extensive research has provided historically accurate captions unseen in other works.

The reader should keep in mind that these photos, whether taken by professionals with superior cameras or by veterans as amateur snapshots, were all created under less than favorable conditions and have suffered first the ravages of the tropics and then the passage of half a century. Action pictures in particular often have obvious flaws in quality. They can not be staged. Some combat photos were made with hand held cameras, but many were taken by fixed cameras mounted in the tail, wing, or nose of various aircraft. The range of fixed cameras was estimated and set prior to takeoff. Once airborne, the camera was activated by the pilot, but he could not adjust for focus nor worry about positioning the target down sun.

Regardless of any imperfections, these rare photos provide a unique visual record of World War II in the Pacific, a conflict wherein air power proved to be the decisive factor.

CONTENTS

1

THE LIBERATION OF LUZON
AND THE SOUTHERN PHILIPPINES

With Leyte secure, if not completely conquered, General Douglas MacArthur's forces turned their attention toward the balance of the Philippines. Mindoro was invaded on 15 December 1944, a prelude to the 9 January 1945 landings at Lingayen Gulf on Luzon. Palawan, Zamboanga, Panay, Negros, Cebu, Bohol, and Mindinao (in that order) were invaded between 28 February and 17 April 1945 without interference from the Japanese navy.

Japanese air units in the Philippines fought the encroaching Allied naval armadas, using Kamikaze tactics in many cases. Both Navy carrier strikes and AAF land-based units concentrated on Japanese airfields and the protection of the fleet, but still the Japanese extracted a heavy toll of ships and crews. In the days between 15 December and 16 January, when the last Japanese air resistance was crushed, the Allies lost 12 ships sunk (one CVE, three cargo vessels, six landing craft and two

mine sweepers) and 61 damaged. Casualties from these ship attacks were heavy.

The Japanese fought street-by-street in Manila, obliging the U.S. Army to destroy most of the old city in a grueling ten-day battle. Other Luzon-based Japanese forces retreated into the rugged Northern Cordillera Mountains and contested that highly defensible terrain until the Imperial Surrender Edict of 15 August 1945.

Once the U.S. Navy had moved north of the Philippines, Fifth Air Force and Marine units were obliged to lend close ground support to an extent never before needed in the Pacific. As Japanese perimeters shrank, however, more AAF and Navy shore-based aircraft arrived in the Philippines to begin turning their attention to enemy bastions and commerce in the South China Sea region. From the Philippine Islands, Borneo, French Indo-China, Formosa, and the China coast came within striking distance.

Task Force 77 CVEs underway in the Philippines on 1 January 1945 to support the invasion of Luzon. (USN)

Above: Ens. George Corthorn, VC-76 from carrier *Kadashan Bay* CVE-76, lands his FM-2 with apparent flak damage to the left aileron. He was engaged in supporting the Lingayen, Luzon, invasion. (USN)

Below: A TBM-3 of VC-84 gets a "sling shot" launch from the catapult of *Makin Island*, CVE-93 during the invasion of Lingayen. (USN)

Ommaney Bay CVE-79 is shown here being consumed by the fires that would sink her off Luzon on 4 January 1945. A Judy pilot crashed the ship with his bomb load, igniting aircraft on the deck that were fueled and armed. Crew losses were 93 killed and 63 wounded. The destroyer *Patterson* is at the right. (USN)

A bomb-carrying Zeke, aflame and being torn by AA fire, is seen just seconds from impact with the port navigating bridge wing of *New Mexico* BB-40. *New Mexico* stayed on station off Luzon but suffered 29 killed and 87 wounded. Among the dead were the ships's Captain, R.W. Fleming, and *Time Magazine* correspondent, William Chickering. (NARS)

A deck officer on *Sangamon* CVE-26 examines flak damage to a VT-37 Avenger. The hole was acquired during Cebu operations. (NARS)

The last Liberator unit assigned to the Pacific was the Seventh Air Force's 494th Bomb Group. Flying from the Palaus, they first took part in attacks on Japanese bases in the Carolines and Philippines early in 1945.

Above: BULL II (left), a B-24M, and SNIFFIN' GRIFFIN (right), a B-24J of the 865th Bomb Squadron with bomb bay doors open. (Bill Hess)

Below: A B-24J named PLAY BOY, of the 867th Bomb Squadron over the Gulf of Davao off Mindinao, P.I. (Bill Hess)

Parachute fragmentation bombs rain down on Clark Field during January 1945 attacks by Fifth Air Force B-25s and A-20s. One twin-engine bomber (lower right) is vulnerable in the open but many more aircraft can be seen dispersed among the trees. (NARS)

A stick of bombs from a 494th Liberator explodes on coastal fortifications on Corregidor Island and walks offshore on 10 February 1945. (Author's Collection)

Douglas A-20s of the 312th Bomb Group worked at very low altitude while bombing and strafing over Luzon.

Above: At Marikina airfield they found Japanese aircraft widely dispersed in bunkers that were camouflaged under bamboo frames. (Authors Collection)

Below: Rolling stock near Legaspi gets, what appears to be, a second going over. (Author's Collection)

The 49th Fighter Group was one of the first to operate out of Lingayen's airfields after the invasion of Luzon. This is the Lightning of Lt. Col. Gerald R. Johnson, a 22-victory ace. The Aussie flag represents a Boomerang that Johnson mistakenly downed in New Guinea. The Australian pilot was unhurt. Johnson was killed in October 1945 enroute to Japan in a flying accident. (Jim Crow)

Several thousand Japanese Navy troops defended Corregidor, in Manila Bay, just as American and Filipino troops had in 1942. It is seen here being bombed by Thirteenth Air Force B-24s prior to invasion. The island was retaken with heavy fighting after a combined parachute-amphibious assault on 16 February 1945. (NARS)

Above: A P-38L of the 431st Squadron, 475th Fighter Group, pilot Floyd Fenton at Lingayen. (Jim Crow)

Below: The Lightning of Lt. Col. Emmett "Cyclone" Davis, CO of the 8th Fighter Group at Mindoro in February 1945. (Jim Crow)

This P-38 of the 347th Fighter Group was only good for spare parts after colliding with a truck on landing. (Jim Crow)

SHOOT YOU'RE LOADED, another 347th P-38, was totaled (left) in a landing accident on Palawan. Its crew chief (right) salvaged the nose art (Jim Crow)

PACIFIC PROWLER and HAWKEYE HATTIE II were P-38s of the 347th Fighter Group. (Jim Crow)

A 12th Squadron, 18th Fighter Group P-38L at Samar, P.I. (Jim Crow)

Pockets of Japanese troops in highly defensible positions held out until the Imperial surrender edict in August. They were attacked with strafing, bombs and Napalm by virtually every aircraft in the Fifth Air Force.

Above: P-38s of the 49th Fighter Group drop tanks filled with Napalm. (USAF)

Right: 58th Fighter Group P-47s sweep in toward a target. (NARS)

A Fifth Air Force P-38 can be seen pulling out of a diving attack over the rugged Cordillera mountains of Northern Luzon, as a smoke ring rises above an explosion. What appear to be steps are rice terraces. (NARS)

1945 marked the beginning of the Mustang era in Fifth Air Force. 35th Fighter Group P-51s taxi for a close support mission against Japanese forces in Northern Luzon. Each carries a pair of 500-pounders. (NARS)

FRENCHY II, was a P-38J of the 7th Squadron, 49th Group, flown by 1st Lt. Joe McHenry. The victory flag represents a Zeke 52 destroyed over Mabalacat, Luzon. (Jim Crow)

Capt. Louis Curdes and the 3rd Air Commandos arrived in the Pacific late in the war. He had flown a previous tour of combat in the Mediterranean, claiming seven German and one Italian aircraft. He downed a Dinah north of Luzon on 10 February 1945 then encountered an American C-47, without a radio, about to land on an enemy occupied island. He expertly shot out one of its engines forcing it to ditch. All passengers and crew were rescued. (NARS)

Night fighters found limited action in the SWP after 1 January 1945. These 419th Night Fighter Squadron P-61 Black Widows roamed from the Philippines to the Netherlands East Indies.

Left: Capt. Ed Grossheider's tiger shark nosed aircraft at Zamboanga, Mindinao. (Jim Crow)

Below: VIVACIOUS VIVIAN at Floridablanca, Luzon. (Author's Collection)

It is estimated that Japanese aircraft losses in the Philippines campaign numbered near 7,000 including Kamikazes. Some of those abandoned on their airfields are shown here and on succeeding pages.

Kawasaki Ki-45 Nick, 45th Hiko Sentai (Author's Collection)

Kawasaki Ki-48 Lily, probably 75th Hiko Sentai. (Author's Collection)

Ki-45 Nick, 27th Hiko Sentai. Much of the damage was caused not by bombing and strafing but by souvenir hunters who hacked at the fabric control surfaces or removed inspection plates. (Author's Collection)

A Mitsubishi G3M-2 Nell, unit unknown. (Author's Collection)

Right: A Nakajima Ki-49 Helen, 74th Hiko Sentai. What appears to be a Maltese cross is a four-leafed seven design. (Author's Collection)

This Mitsubishi Ki-21 Sally, unit unknown, was being towed to a protective revetment near San Manuel, Luzon, when strafers attacked. Both tug and aircraft were disabled. (NARS)

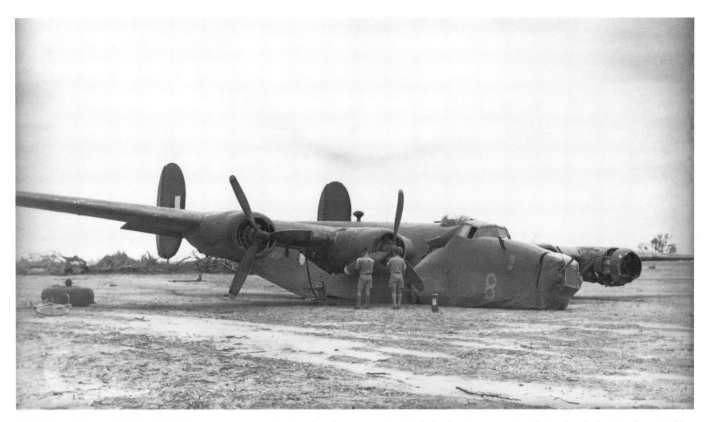

In 1945, as Fifth and Thirteenth Air Forces moved north, the Aussies concentrated their air offense on the Netherlands East Indies. RAAF was largely equipped with American made aircraft, early bombers being transfers from AAF units.

Above: HELL'S BELLE, a modified B-24D veteran of the 90th Bomb Group, Fifth Air Force, joined the RAAF and came to the end of the road in this January 1945 crash landing at Tucomwal. (Bob Livingstone)

Below: RAAF Liberators ranged far over the Netherlands East Indies from bases in Northwest Australia. Here a B-24L of 24 Squadron RAAF returns to Truscott from an 8 February 1945 raid on the Kali Kontan power station in Southeast Java, Netherlands East Indies. (Bob Livingstone)

After helping to subdue Japanese forces in the Philippines, Fifth AF Mitchells and Havocs turned their attention toward installations on Formosa and South China Sea traffic.

Above: A B-25J, SN 43-36016 of the 345th Bomb Group at Lingayen. (Author's Collection)

Below: An A-20 of the 312th Bomb Group. This Havoc completed 126 missions. (Author's Collection)

Left: This 1,600 ton freighter was found off the China coast and sunk by 345th Bomb Group Mitchells on 1 March 1945. (NARS)

Below: On 21 March 1945 the 345th caught a small convoy off the coast of French Indo-China and dispatched several vessels including this 2,000 ton tanker. (NARS)

Long-range Navy PB4Y-1 Liberators were renowned for their solo armed reconnaissance exploits. Philippine-based VPB-117 Liberators came in various models.

Above: DOC'S DELIGHT, Bureau No. 38746, was a J Model with the Erco bow turret. (Bob Livingstone)

Below: DICK'S DIXIE, Bureau No. 65298, was a rare NMF L Model Lib with an Erco nose turret. (Bob Livingstone)

The shadow of Lt. J.H. Burton's Liberator can be seen on 28 February 1945 as the PB4Y-1 of VPB-104 attacks a coastal lugger. This action occurred near the Ryukyu Islands. (NARS)

A Sally of the 16th Hiko Sentai command flight was encountered and downed by Lt. George Waldeck's PB4Y-1 of VPB-104 in the East China Sea on 5 March 1945. (NARS)

Right: A 200 ton freighter was found off Swatow, China on 6 March 1945 by Lt. Stan Wood's PB4Y-1 of VPB-104. It was sunk and the its deck cargo of barrels was set adrift. (NARS)

On 22 March 1945 the PB4Y-1 of Lt. A.G. Elder, VPB-117 was over Borneo hunting targets ashore or afloat when to their surprise, a Nakajima B5N lifted off a runway. The Lib did a 180 degree turn and pursued the Kate. It is seen here at very low altitude, gear still extended, as it attempts to return to the airfield. The bow, top and starboard waist gunners combined to down the enemy plane. (NARS)

Lt. Ray Ettinger and his VPB-104 crew conduct a lone attack on Koshun AD, Formosa on 27 March 1945. The gunners on the PB4Y-1 Liberator strafed Nates, Kates and Jill aircraft in protective revetments. (NARS)

A 2,300 ton tanker under attack off French Indo-China on 29 March 1945. A direct hit by 1st Lt. John Loisel, 500th Squadron, 345th Bomb Group caused this ship to sink. (NARS)

The PB4Y-1 of Lt. Cdr. Whitney Wright, VB-104, took these photos during March 1945 shipping attacks off the China coast.

Above: A small tanker is dead in the water and possibly aground near Amoy. The Liberator attack has started a fire and and fractured a tank that leaks crude oil. (NARS)

Below: This 2,000 ton freighter escaped with some damage. Note the AA guns above the bridge. (NARS)

While hunting west of Formosa, near the island of Quemoy on 6 April 1945, B-25s from the 345th Bomb Group attacked a pair of Japanese patrol-escort vessels (similar to USN DEs).

Above: The camera snapped just as this ship, believed to be Type C, No. 1, took a direct hit from a 500-pounder dropped by the aircraft of Capt. George Musket. (NARS)

Below: A Type D, No. 134, was also sunk by the combined bombs and machine guns of the Mitchells. (NARS)

PV-1 Venturas of VPB-137 ranged far and wide during May 1945.

Above: Bombing a Butanol plant on Formosa (NARS)

Below: An explosion from a chemical plant on Borneo as seen by the gunner in the ventral turret. (NARS)

On 31 May 1945 a pair of VPB-106 PB4Y-2 Privateers conducted an 11-hour, 1050-mile reconnaissance of Singapore, searching for remnants of the Imperial Fleet.

Above: Near the target they were intercepted by three Oscars and a Zeke and fought them off. The PB4Y of Lt. Cdr. H.F. Mears, Bureau No. 59563, is seen here from Lt. Cdr. G.C. Goodloe's aircraft. Mears aircraft received strikes from an Oscar and a 20mm cannon hit in the No. 3 engine from the Zeke. (NARS)

Below: Proceeding back toward, Palawan, P.I., fire soon began to show from Mears right wing, and the No. 4 engine was seen to be cutting out as the Privateer began a rapid loss of altitude. After a time Mears radioed Goodloe, "I'm sorry, but I'm going to have to ditch. Thanks for the way you stuck with me." At about 500 feet the fire in the starboard engine apparently burned through and most of the wing broke off. Goodloe's crew watched helplessly as the Privateer hit the water and exploded. There were no survivors. (NARS)

Above: A Thirteenth Air Force Liberator goes to low level to attack shipping in the Netherlands East Indies in May 1945. (NARS)

Below: A B-25J of the 42nd Bomb Group on a low level run over Victoria Harbor, North Borneo in June 1945. Pilot of this Thirteenth AF strafer was 2nd Lt. Russell Brown. (NARS)

B-24s of the 23rd Squadron, 5th Bomb Group, a veteran Thirteenth Air Force unit, over Balikpapen, Borneo, 2 July 1945. Nearest Lib is TOP O' THE MARK, SN 44-42245, a dash M model. Below is the Allied invasion fleet. (A.W. James via Fred Johnsen)

P-38Ls of the 475th Fighter Group ranged from Luzon to China with 300 and 165 gal. spare tanks. (AFM)

By mid-1945, the Liberator was in the twilight of its war service. Many AAF B-24 groups did not advance beyond the Philippines or Marianas because their targets were limited, airfield space on Okinawa was at a premium, and the B-29 had assumed the long-range strategic bombing role. But the slab-sided Liberator was the ultimate "canvas" for nose art. Several examples are displayed on this and succeeding pages.

The Woodward crew pose next to their B-24J, SN 42-73147, BOMBS TO NIP ON. They were with the 394th Squadron, 5th Bomb Group. (NARS)

B-24J, SN 42-73489, 531st Squadron, 380th Bomb Group. (Author's Collection)

B-24, of the 43rd Bomb Group. (Author's Collection)

B-24J, SN 42-109986, 528th Squadron, 380th Bomb Group. (Author's Collection)

B-24J, SN 44-40429, 64th Squadron, 43rd Bomb Group. (Author's Collection)

B-24J, SN 44-41077, 22nd Bomb Group, with group logo. (Author's Collection)

B-24L, SN 44-41698, 72nd Squadron, 5th Bomb Group. (Author's Collection)

B-24J, SN 44-40543, 5th Bomb Group. (Author's Collection)

B-24L, SN 44-41480, served with both 5th and 307th Bomb Groups (Author's Collection)

B-24J, SN 42-64053, 6th Photo Recon Group. (Author's Collection)

B-24J, SN 44-40752, 865th Squadron, 494th Bomb Group. (Author's Collection)

B-24J, SN 44-40620, 72nd Squadron, 5th Bomb Group. (Author's Collection)

B-24J, SN 44-40535, 424th Squadron, 307th Bomb Group. (Author's Collection)

B-24J, SN 42-64051, 2nd Squadron, 6th Photo Recon Group. (Author's Collection)

B-24J, SN 44-40335, 403rd Squadron, 43rd Bomb Group on Los Negros Is., P.I. (Jim Crow)

B-24J, SN 44-40428, 64th Squadron, 43rd Bomb Group. (Ernie McDowell)

B-24J, SN 44-40729, 867th Squadron, 494th Bomb Group. (Author's Collection)

B-24J, SN 42-73044, 2nd Squadron, 6th Photo Recon Group. (Author's Collection)

B-24J, SN 44-40715, 864th Squadron, 494th Bomb Group. (Author's Collection)

B-24J, SN 44-40683, 392nd Squadron, 30th Bomb Group, Madsall crew. (Author's Collection)

B-24J, SN 44-40760, 867th Squadron, 494th Bomb Group, Bill Lambert, AC. (Author's Collection)

2

CARRIER STRIKES FROM INDO-CHINA TO JAPAN

After supporting Luzon landing operations, the U.S. Third Fleet's Task Force 38 (with 13 fast carriers) turned its attention to raiding Formosa, the most likely source of Philippine reinforcements, then struck deep across the South China Sea to French Indo-China and the China mainland. As the Third Fleet retired for rest, repair, and replenishment it was relieved by the Fifth Fleet and Task Force 58. At this point in the war the U.S. Navy had 18 CVs and CVLs in the Pacific.

Such was the wealth of Allied carrier air power at the start of 1945, that a Royal Navy task force, freed from conflicts on the other side of the globe, joined the Pacific war in February 1945. It included four aircraft carriers (a fifth would be added), two battleships, six cruisers, fifteen destroyers, and its own support fleet. En route from India to Australia the Royal Navy raided the oil refinery at Palembang, Sumatra on 4 January.

Led by Vice Admiral Mitscher, the fast carriers of Task Force 58 ventured far to the north on 16 February 1945, conducting strikes against Japanese bases on Honshu near Tokyo. This was the first naval approach to the Japanese homeland since the Doolittle raid of April 1942. These operations were a prelude to the invasion of Iwo Jima, a long-held Japanese possession, just 650 miles south of Honshu. Such was the depleted state of the Imperial Navy that they failed to contest these forays into home waters.

The Vought Corsair had been designed as a carrier-based fighter, but was shore-based until late 1944. VMF-124 and VMF-213 began combat operations from *Essex* with 3 January 1945 raids on Formosa. (USN)

41

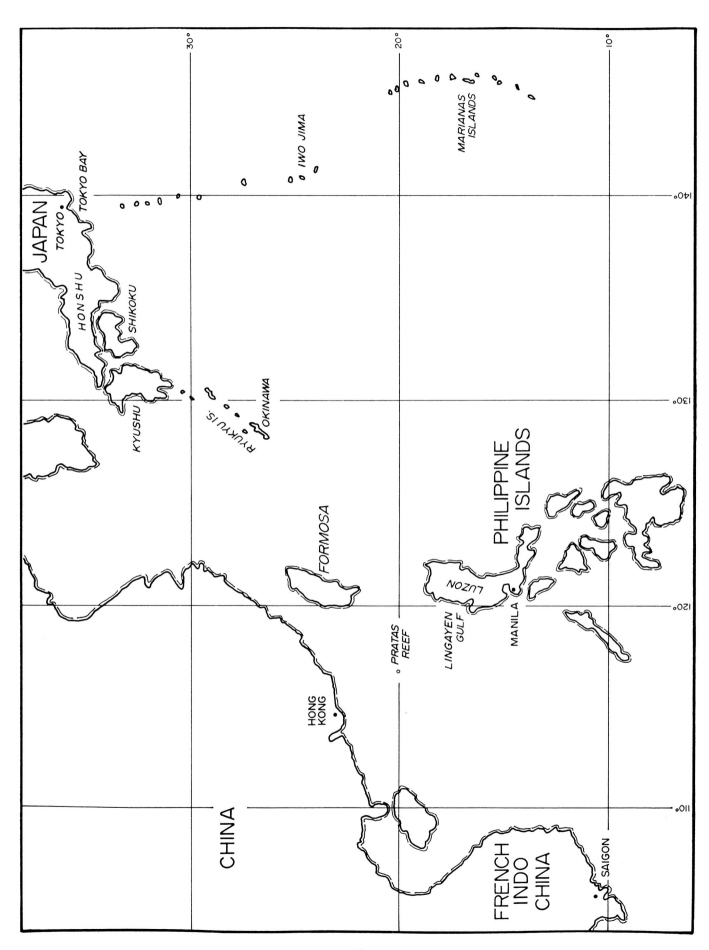

JAPAN

TOKYO

TOKYO BAY

HONSHU

SHIKOKU

KYUSHU

RYUKYU IS.

OKINAWA

IWO JIMA

MARIANAS ISLANDS

CHINA

FORMOSA

PRATAS REEF

HONG KONG

LINGAYEN GULF

LUZON

MANILA

PHILIPPINE ISLANDS

FRENCH INDO CHINA

SAIGON

30°

20°

10°

140°

130°

120°

110°

A Marine F4U-1D, hook extended, takes the wire on *Essex*. (USMC)

Corsairs of VMF-124 from *Essex* escorted TBM Avengers of VT-4 to Formosa on the 3 January 1945 raid. The strike force was intercepted by a twin-engine Frances and downed by Lt. Col. William Millington. It was the first claim for ship-based Marines. (MNA)

Left: Pilots of *Lexington*'s VT-20 exchange views after the Formosa mission. (L. to r.) Lt. (jg) Robert D. Olson, Lt. (jg) Herbert A. Koster, Ens. John J McIntosh, and Lt. (jg) W.C. Pohtilla. Olson and Koster were killed in action during subsequent operations. As Pacific airmen came within range of China they all wore the CBI patch on their flight suits, identifying them to mainland guerrillas as friendly in case they were downed over China.

Below: The Hellcat of Lt. (jg) Rolan D. Powell of VF-3 was downed during the Formosa strike. He was rescued and is shown here being returned to *Yorktown* from *Cassin Young* DD-793 via breeches buoy. (USN)

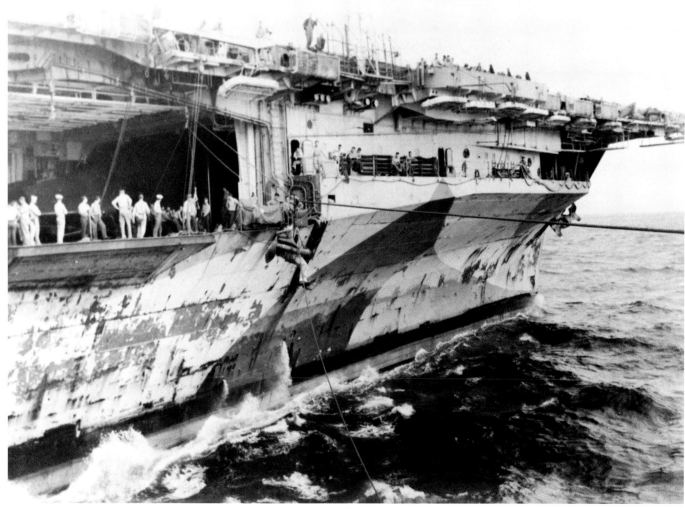

Aircraft from *Hornet* CV-12 were involved in strikes on Japanese air bases on Luzon on 5 January 1945.

Above: An F6F is man handled into position on the flight deck. (MNA)

Right: VF and VBF-17 Hellcats prepare for launching. (MNA)

Task Force 38, seeking the Japanese surface fleet that had escaped the Philippines, struck deep into the South China Sea in January, penetrating to the coast of French Indo-China. The Imperial Navy's battle force was absent, but two convoys of merchantmen with escorts were discovered and subjected to two attacks.

Above: This photo of four ships burning and sinking was taken by an aircraft from *Lexington*. (USN)

Below: The largest naval escort with the convoys was light cruiser *Kashii,* seen here sinking by the stern. Attacked by VT-20 and VB-20, she took three torpedo and several bomb hits but downed one TBM and one F6F with AA fire. (NARS)

Above: TBM-1C Avengers of VT-4 from *Essex* departing Saigon on 12 January 1945 after striking oil storage facilities, docks and ships at anchor. (MNA)

Below: A Curtiss SB2C-3 Helldiver of VB-7 (foreground) is escorted by a VF-7 Hellcat. The shipping attacks sank 44 vessels including 15 naval escorts. (NARS)

Both men and aircraft of Air Group 44 strain to stay aboard *Langley* CVL-27 during January heavy weather in the South China Sea. (USN)

SB2C-3 Helldivers of VB-80 from *Ticonderoga CV-19*. *Ticonderoga* sustained heavy damage from a Kamikaze on 21 January 1945 and retired to Ulithi for repairs. Air Group 80 transferred to *Hancock* to complete their tour of duty in March 1945. (Jim Crow)

Carrier aviation is an inherently dangerous occupation, and operational accidents took nearly as many lives as combat.

Above: A landing F6F from VF-30 missed all the arresting gear as another Hellcat is slow in taxiing forward. (MNA)

Below: The barrier wires not being raised, the landing aircraft overtakes the other for a fatal crash The incident took place north of Ulithi on 11 February 1945 as *Belleau Wood*, CVL-24 sailed toward combat. (MNA)

On 16-17 February 1945 Task Force 58 approached to within 60 miles of Honshu and sent two days of wave attacks against Japanese airdromes and aircraft plants in the Tokyo area. Japanese air defenses resisted and there was heavy air combat. The Navy claimed over 500 aircraft destroyed in the air and on the ground, along with heavy damage to a pair of Nakajima plants. Task Force 58 suffered the loss of 60. VF-3, led by Lt. Cdr. Edward Bayers, prepares to launch from *Yorktown*. The Hellcats are armed with 5-inch high velocity rockets. VF-3 claimed 18 victories for the two days. (USN)

A Corsair of VF-84 launches from *Bunker Hill* CV-17 for the Tokyo raids. This was the first combat for the new squadron, led by Lt. Cdr. Roger Hedrick, a Solomons ace with VF-17. They claimed 11 kills in the Tokyo operation. (USN)

Above: During the Tokyo strikes VF-17 from *Hornet* claimed seven aerial kills. The squadron was on its second tour of combat (previously flying F4Us in the Solomons) and was led by Lt. Cdr. Marshall Beebe. VF-17's record of 313 victories made them the Navy's highest-scoring fighter squadron. Here an F6F-5 taxis into position on *Hornet*. (Author's Collection)

Right: Air Group 9, flying from *Lexington*, participated in the 16-17 February 1945 air strikes on targets in the Tokyo area. They were led by Lt. Cdr. Herb Houck on his second tour of combat with VF-9. Houck scored his sixth confirmed victory on 17 February but was killed in that action. (Author's Collection)

An F4U-1D Corsair of VMF-221 approaches *Bunker Hill* for a landing with gear, flaps, and tail hook down. (NARS)

Lt. (JG) Henry Rowland of VF-3 took a cannon direct hit on the tail of his F6F on 17 February 1945 over Tokyo but returned safely for a landing on *Yorktown* CV-10. He claimed destruction of a Tojo. (MNA)

An excellent look at the catapult mechanism, as a VF-80 Hellcat prepares to be launched from *Hancock* in in February 1945. The pilot has his head back, according to the accepted practice, awaiting the catapult officer's signal, (USN)

San Jacinto was one of the carriers of Task Force 58 involved in February 1945 raids on the Bonins and Honshu. Here an Avenger of VT-45 returns, hooking on the last arresting cable. (USN)

Ens. Aaron R. Ives, VF-9, landed long on *Lexington* on 25 February 1945, hitting the barrier and jolting his auxiliary tank loose. It was struck by the prop, and spilled fuel was ignited.

Above: He unbuckles and climbs from the cockpit of his Hellcat. (USN)

Below: Using the wing as an avenue of escape, he eludes the fire. Deck crews quickly suppressed the flames, but the F6F was a loss. (USN)

San Jacinto recovers her brood during Okinawa operations in March 1945. An F6F of VF-45 is waved off after a high approach. (USN)

The U.S. Navy ran into an old adversary, *Yamato* during a 19 March 1945 strike against Inland Sea of Japan targets. The super battleship was underway near Kure, and while damaging hits were claimed by Task Force 58, the big ship survived again. (NARS)

On 19 March 1945 *Franklin* CV-13 was sailing with Task Force 58 off Japan. Air Group 5 was preparing to launch a mission to Kagoshima, Kyushu, when a single undetected Japanese bomber flew the length of the deck dropping a pair of bombs. One hit among the loaded aircraft on the stern deck and the other hit abreast the bridge, blowing out the forward elevator. Fires raged above and below decks as exploding aircraft, rockets, bombs, and .50 cal. ammunition added to the carnage. Casualties were appalling, but the gallant crew saved their ship and returned her to the States. Above: *Franklin* lists heavily to starboard as the cruiser *Santa Fe* comes alongside to render assistance. Casualties among the carrier's crew and air group were over 700 killed and 300 wounded. (USN)

3

VICTORY IN BURMA — STALEMATE IN CHINA

The China-Burma-India theatre of operations was at the tail end of the Allies' longest logistical pipeline, remaining so throughout World War II. For most of the war all military supplies had to be flown from India to China over the Himalaya Mountains, a route airmen designated "The Hump." Because of this, and the fact that there were substantial Japanese ground forces on the Asian mainland, progress was slow compared with Pacific Island campaigns.

After pushing the Japanese back from Imphal in 1943, Allied armies drove them from Northern Burma, in operations utilizing troops that infiltrated or were air-lifted behind enemy lines. These long-range penetration teams were dependent on support and supply from the air. The composite air units established for this type of operation were the Air Commandos.

In Burma the Japanese gave ground grudgingly, fighting desperate actions in a land that favored defense, but by mid-1944 a new overland route — the Ledo Road — connected India and Western China. Still the Ledo road could only carry a trickle of supplies, and massive air transport operations over the Himalayas continued to keep China and the Fourteenth Air Force in the fight.

Despite these problems, the Allies determined to utilize a new strategic air weapon — the Boeing B-29 – from China bases. This aircraft held the hope of striking Japan and other, heretofore untouched targets. Airfields, to accommodate the giant aircraft, had to be built by peasant labor and supplied by air. B-29 Superfortresses arrived in mid-1944 forming the Twentieth Bomber Command. Each B-29 had to participate in the logistical buildup, flying "Hump" missions to stockpile, bombs, gasoline and other essentials.

The first B-29 combat missions were flown in June 1944, including raids against Yawata and Sasebo on Kyushu. Successive raids hit Sasebo and Nagasaki, but each effort required a refueling at advanced Chinese air bases. Losses were limited, but the results from these monumental efforts were considered minimal.

The Japanese were nonetheless alarmed at the intrusion over their homeland, and determined to conduct an overland campaign to take the fields that springboarded the B-29s. Moving south from Hankow and north from Canton, Japanese ground forces had driven along a rail corridor across the heart of China by November 1944, seizing or enveloping many Allied airfields. Major General Claire Chennault's air forces maintained air supremacy but, despite their best efforts at supporting the Chinese Army, they could not prevent the loss of several advanced airfields. As Allied advanced bases were abandoned, precious fuel and other material that had been laboriously hauled over the Hump had to be destroyed. Pushed back into China, Twentieth Bomber Command concentrated its effort on Southeast Asian targets such as Formosa, Manchuria, Singapore, and Bangkok.

Meanwhile, with RAF and the AAF's Tenth Air Force in support, the British Army had driven Japanese forces south through Burma. Rangoon fell on 3 May 1945. Although the ground situation in China had reached a frustrating stalemate, Pacific amphibious advances had provided an option for the strategic bombing campaign. In March 1945 B-29s of Twentieth Bomber Command abandoned the China experiment for fields that had been prepared in the Marianas Islands, there to concentrate on Japan. They had flown just 49 missions in eleven months. The underequipped and undersupplied Fourteenth Air Force continued to exercise air supremacy over China, but without any hope of advance. The CBI had fallen into the backwash of the Pacific war.

Maj. Gen. Claire Chennault, commander of the Flying Tigers and later the Fourteenth Air Force (far right) poses with some of his leaders as they display the Fourteenth banner: (l. to r.) Brig. Gen. Clinton Vincent, 6-victory ace and head of the China Air Task Force, Maj. Albert Baumler, 23rd Fighter Group ace, Col. (later General) Bruce K. Holloway, 13-victory ace and CO 23rd Fighter Group, Col. Henry E. Strickland, Fourteenth AF Adjutant, and Chennault. (USAF)

Maj. John "Pappy" Herbst served with and finally commanded the 74th Squadron, 23rd Fighter Group. He few both the Curtiss P-40 and the P-51 in combat, scoring 18 victories. He was killed in a 1946 flying accident. (Author's Collection)

Above: A P-51A of the 1st Air Commandos. (NARS)

Below: The Bomber Section of the 1st Air Commandos was equipped with the 75mm cannon B-25H. (NARS) Led by Col. Philip Cochran, the unit supported the aerial invasion of Northern Burma.

The 459th Fighter Squadron, Tenth Air Force was one of just three scattered P-38 units in the CBI.

Above: Maj. Willard J. Webb in his Lightning. He claimed five aerial and three ground kills. (Jim Crow)

Right: The pilot of this P-38J of the 459th apparently had a bleak outlook on the war from his vantage point in the CBI. It was named GOLDEN GATE IN '48?. (Jim Crow)

The 311th Fighter Group joined the Tenth Air Force in India late in 1943. It transferred to the Fourteenth Air Force in China a year later. Its original equipment was the P-51A Mustang, shown here with 500-pounders at Dinjin, Assam. (Authors Collection)

Capt. Sidney Newcomb of the 530th Squadron, 311th Fighter Group, was credited with four kills and one probable in his P-51A, the last victory was over Rangoon. (Jim Crow)

A tight formation of Tenth Air Force Thunderbolts over the rugged Burmese hill country early in 1945. (NARS)

A Tenth Air Force P-47D Thunderbolt of the 90th Squadron, 80th Fighter Group, armed with a pair of 500 lb. bombs. (NARS)

The old and the new meet at Cox's Bazar on the Bay of Bengal, Assam, India early in 1945. Foreground is PITT'S POT, the P-47D of Capt. Younger Pitts, CO of the 6th Fighter Squadron, 1st Air Commando Group. In the background is a newly arrived P-51D of the 2nd Air Commando Group. (Ted Young)

Beginning in 1944 the Royal Air Force in the CBI began converting their Hurricane and Spitfire units to the Republic Thunderbolt. By 1945 they fielded ten squadrons in Burma. Here a No. 135 Squadron Thunderbolt II with a pair of 165 gal. tanks lifts off. (Jerry Scutts)

Above: GUN TOTIN' DEACON, a 341st Bomb Group B-25D, was badly bent after its nose wheel collapsed on landing. (NARS)

Left: Delayed action 500-pounders, with spikes screwed into the nose, were tried by low-level B-25 Mitchells to cut rail lines. At low-level bombs tended to bounce off the target. This method proved to be no more effective than other techniques. The farm field to the right of the rail line had been potholed by a stick of bombs dropped from high altitude.(NARS)

Right: 308th Bomb Group Liberators attack a Japanese supply depot in the Changsha area of China from high altitude. (NARS)

With the long supply line from India, transports had more than their share of mishaps. This Curtiss C-46, CARGO PACKIN' MAMA, had a hydraulic problem, forcing a belly landing at Kunming, China. (NARS)

Above: With Fourteenth Air Force P-40s providing close escort, B-24s of the 308th Bomb Group conduct a strike on Japanese installations at Sinshih. (NARS)

Below: 1st Lt. Don S. Lopez, an ace with the 75th Squadron, 23rd Fighter Group, was taxiing this old P-40 when it took a bite out of one of the new P-51s. Lopez flew both the Warhawk and the Mustang. (Author's Collection)

Above: A recon version of the B-24, an F-7A of the 8th Photo Recon Group, at Dum Dum air base, Calcutta, India. (Jim Crow)

Below: GEORGIA PEACH, was a B-24J, SN 42-73445, of the Fourteenth Air Force's 308th Bomb Group. Symbols above the nose art are for 30 bombing missions, and the flag is for a Japanese interceptor claimed by the crew. Symbols to the right are barrels representing supply mission. (Jim Crow)

A pair of bedraggled China American Composite Wing veterans show their teeth during maintenance at Peishiyi, China.

Above: This worn P-40N crashed on take-off shortly after posing. (Jim Crow)

Below: A P-51B stands stands near a new Dash D. (Jim Crow)

A mixture of Chinese and AAF crews were combined to form the Chinese American Composite Wing (CACW).

Above: A B-25H of the 1st Bomb Squadron, CACW gets pre-flighted by its crew chief-gunner, Sgt. Ken Daniels. The Dash H was equipped with a 75mm cannon that was primarily used against rail targets. Forward fixed armament also included eight .50 caliber machine guns. (Ken Daniels)

Below: A new B-25J of the CACW's 1st Bomb Squadron over China in 1945. (Ken Daniels)

Cutting Japanese supply routes was a primary task in the CBI. Since there were few roads away from coastal area, rail lines were the principle means of surface communication.

Above: This bridge over the Yen Do Canal in French Indo-China had been previously damaged and was under repair when visited on 5 March 1945 by 341st Bomb Group B-25s. Note the bomb, tumbling away from the Mitchell, just left of center. (NARS)

Below: The Ha Trung rail bridge in French Indo-China is put out of business by 341st Bomb Group Mitchells on 31 March 1945. (NARS)

Both Mitchells and Liberators of the Fourteenth Air Force hunted shipping in the South China Sea.

Right: A freighter begins to burn aft after an attack by 308th Bomb Group B-24s. (NARS)

Below: Bombs straddle a cargo ship during an attack by 341st Bomb Group B-25s. (NARS)

The logistical difficulty faced by the Twentieth Bomber Command in its ill-fated China operations is clearly exhibited by the mission marks on these two 462nd Bomb Group B-29s. Each bomb painted on the nose represents a combat mission, and each camel shows a supply flight over the Himalayas.

Above: The Whitfield crew in OLD-BITCH-U-AIRY BESS, SN42-6270, had flown three missions vs. 15 supply runs. (Author's Collection)

Below: The Terwilliger crew in CASE ACE, SN42-6273, had managed just one mission for five Hump trips. Both photos were taken in November 1944. (Author's Collection)

Above: The Mukden, Manchuria mission of 7 December 1944 encountered a strong Japanese air defense. Seven B-29s were lost including No. 42-63395 of the 468th Bomb Group. Low on fuel and weighted down with ice, she crashed on landing in China. (NARS)

Below: On 24 February 1945 B-29s raided the Empire Docks of Singapore at the Southern tip of Malaya. Despite severe flak damage to this 40th Bomb Group Superfort, her crew returned to base. (NARS)

The destruction of most Japanese air power in the CBI made for sparse hunting for AAF night fighters.

Above: Black Widows of the 426th Night Fighter Squadron scored just five victories over China in eleven months of operations. (Jim Crow)

Below: Arriving in Burma in late 1944, 427th P-61s had no intercepts but conducted their own night intruder operations. They also carried rockets and bombs in operations over Burma. (Jim Crow)

By 1945 the 311th Fighter Group had progressed through B and C model Mustangs to P-51Ds of the 530th Squadron, shown here over China in August 1945. (NARS)

TOUGH TITTI, a B-24J SN 44-40296 of the 308th Bomb Group is seen from another Liberator's waist gun window over Hong Kong. (Wally Forman)

A 75mm cannon-equipped B-25H of the 12th Bomb Group over Southern Burma early in 1945. (Author's collection)

Grumman Hellcat IIs of the Royal Navy 808 Squadron are shown here being armed with rockets aboard HMS *Khedive* in mid-1945, as the Royal Navy's East Indies Fleet supported amphibious operations in Burma. (Jerry Scutts)

4

THE LAST BEACHHEADS: IWO JIMA & OKINAWA

Long before the Philippines had been secured, Allied strategy had focused on using the Marianas as a base for the strategic bombing of Japan. A logical extension of that strategy dictated the invasion of Iwo Jima. The distance between the Marianas and Tokyo was approximately 1,300 miles. Iwo Jima in the Bonin Islands — midway to Japan — was 650 miles from Honshu and had two airfields. It represented not only a haven for disabled B-29s returning from Japan, but would provide a base for AAF fighter escorts. Therefore, as early as mid-1944 General Hap Arnold had suggested the seizure of this seemingly modest piece of real estate.

Iwo Jima had been subjected to carrier strikes, routinely bombed by Seventh Air Force heavies for months and appeared battered. Its few square miles were then totally denuded by two days of pre-invasion bombardment. Just prior to D-Day, the invasion task force drenched the island with over 31,000 large caliber shells. Yet the invasion of 19 February 1945 proved to be costly for the Marines. The Japanese had constructed reinforced concrete defenses deep into Iwo Jima's sulfuric soil. Its 21,000 defenders fought to near annihilation for six weeks, extracting over 6,000 killed and more than 17,000 wounded from Marine ranks.

Less than two months later the Allied invasion armada, now numbering 1,213 ships and over 560 carrier aircraft, approached the Ryukyu Islands for the next and final amphibious assault of the Pacific war — Okinawa. Much larger than most other volcanic islands of the Pacific, Okinawa has 485 square miles of rugged terrain. Once again, the Japanese had anticipated invasion and built defenses in depth. Carrier strikes and a pre-invasion bombardment of historic proportions did little to diminish the underground defensive network. Okinawa was invaded on 1 April 1945 and fought over until July. Casualties among the joint Army-Marine assault force were over 7,600 killed and nearly 32,000 wounded; the heaviest of the Pacific war.

The tired P-47D Thunderbolts of the 318th Fighter Group had neutralized all of the uninvaded Marianas with bombs, rockets and .50 caliber bullets, but they did not have the range to reach targets beyond. Seventh AF Liberators paid periodic visits to Iwo Jima, but the 318th could only provide escort to within 40 miles of Iwo. Truk was even further beyond the Jug's range. (Author's Collection)

Above: In order to solve the long-range escort problem, three dozen Lightnings were dispatched from Hawaii to augment the 318th Fighter Group late in 1944. This P-38L belonged to Maj. John Hussey, CO of the 73rd Squadron. He downed a Zeke on one of the early escort missions to Truk. This view shows the P-38's four .50s and single 20mm protruding from the nose. (Author's Collection)

Left: The Jim Hewett crew of the 819th Squadron, 30th Bomb Group were veterans of the long-range missions to Truk and Iwo. Their B-24, SN44-40527 was a J model. (Author's Collection)

78

Above: ITCHY BITCH, a P-38L of the 318th Fighter Group, is shown here with crew chief, Sgt. Fred Sofio. While flown by 1st Lt. Bill Eustis, this P-38 chased a Zeke over Truk, had a mid-air collision, and Eustis became a POW. (Author's Collection)

Below: Maj. Warren Roeser, 318th Fighter Group, bagged one recon aircraft over Saipan, a Zeke over Pagan, and an Oscar over Iwo Jima. (Author's Collection)

Above: On 27 January 1945 the B-24J, PATRIOTIC PATTY, 392nd Squadron, 30th Bomb Group, received a direct hit in the cockpit from a heavy AA gun over Iwo. Both the pilot, 1st Lt. Herbert Broemer, and the co-pilot were severely wounded, the instrument panel was destroyed, the auto-pilot was out, and the hydraulic system was damaged. Despite injuries to one eye and one arm, Broemer got the plane under control and with the assistance of other crew members, brought them home to Saipan landing at 100 mph. (NARS)

As the long-planned invasion of Iwo Jima approached, Seventh Air Force reconnaissance aircraft began mapping the island. Above: An F-5A (unarmed Lightning) of the 28th Photo Recon Squadron. (Author's Collection)

Mapping terrain and defenses just a few days before the invasion, an F-5 of the 28th Photo Recon Squadron races low across Iwo Jima. In this oblique camera frame, the photo plane captured both a wrecked Oscar (minus engine) and an escorting P-38 of the 318th Fighter Group (upper right). (NARS)

During a 318th Fighter Group low-level sweep over Iwo, 1st Lt. Fred Erbele took cannon hits on his right wing and left engine on 5 January 1945. After nearly crashing, and with speed down to 120 mph, he managed to get the P-38L stabilized, then gained some altitude to parachute. But being far from any rescue units, he opted to continue on one engine toward Saipan. With his speed up to 135 mph and altitude of about 3,000 feet, he was mothered along by a B-24 and landed after 8 3/4 hours.

Left: The hole in the right wing. Erbele is in the center without a cap. (Author's Collection)

Left: A view of the damaged left engine minus the the prop spinner that was blown off. During the Okinawa campaign, Fred Eberle was again hit by flak, parachuted, and was rescued by a PBM flying boat. (Author's Collection)

Right: Navy patrol squadrons also ranged out from the Marianas on missions described as "offensive search and reconnaissance." This PB4Y-1, Lt. (jg) Francis Burton, AC, flying from Tinian, downed a Mitsubishi Betty near Iwo Jima. The crew was assigned to VPB-102. (Hal Olsen)

Right: While escorting photo recon aircraft to Iwo Jima on 3 February 1945 1st Lt. Robert Amon, 318th Fighter Group took a hit from AA that nearly severed his right tail boom. Lacking right rudder controls, he still managed to fly his P-38 back to Saipan. (NARS)

Task Force 58's fast carriers joined in attacks on Iwo Jima and other Japanese bases in the Bonin Islands just before the invasion.

Above: An *Essex* Hellcat of VF-83 returns from CAP its arresting hook snagging a wire. (MNA)

Below: A VT-17 TBM-3 recovers on *Bunker Hill* with flak damage apparent in both wings. (MNA)

Right up to the invasion of Iwo Jima the Japanese maintained a small fighter force. This Oscar, damaged by carrier strikes or P-38 attacks, was found and picked over by souvenir hunters after the island was taken. (Author's Collection)

As the Allied invasion armada approached Iwo Jima on 16 February 1945, cruiser *Pensacola* launched one of its OS2U Kingfisher scouts. It was engaged by what may have been Iwo's last operational Japanese fighter. Lt.(jg) Douglas W. Gandy was directing the ship's bombardment when a Zeke 52 made a pass at him. Gandy gamely followed, managed to bring his plane about 500 feet astern of the Zeke and banged away with his single fixed .30 caliber machine gun. To Gandy's surprise, a stream of smoke appeared, the enemy aircraft slowed, and then began to turn. Gandy gave it another burst then watched as it half-rolled, burst into flames and crashed on the island. (Ray Snapp)

D-Day, 19 February 1945, an aerial view of the amphibious landing on Iwo Jima. The giant ship in the center is BB *North Carolina*, and the small white wakes are made by waves of landing craft. This dramatic photo was taken by an F6F-5P from *Bunker Hil's* VF-84. (MNA)

Right: On D+1 a TBM (unit unknown) is hit by AA fire and goes down near the invasion fleet. (Author's Collection)

Below: The black volcanic sand of Red Beach on Iwo Jima is a scene of chaos. Beached landing craft and hastily dumped supplies are apparent despite the smoke of battle. The ship at center right is Japanese, hit and grounded by an earlier carrier strike. (Author's Collection)

Continuous close support for the Marines ashore was provided by fourteen CVEs of Task Force 52. In many cases the VC squadron strikes were directed at locations on map grids, since identifiable strong points on the surface of Iwo had been reduced or were impossible to discern from the air due to the below-surface structures

Above: A TBM-3 from VC-79 of *Sargent Bay* CVE-83, prepares to launch. (USN)

Below: FM-2 Wildcats from *Sargent Bay,* armed with rockets, add their firepower to the infantry support. (USN)

The venerable *Saratoga* CV-3 was providing CAP for the Iwo Jima invasion force on 21 February 1945 when a flight of six determined Japanese naval aviators, attacked. A combination of bombs and crashing aircraft quickly turned *Saratoga* into an inferno. Here her crew can be seen battling the fires that raged forward. She survived but suffered 123 killed and 192 wounded and was out of operations for three months. (USN)

For several days after D-Day, Task Force 58 hovered in the Iwo Jima region to protect against any intrusion by the Japanese fleet and to hammer outlying Bonin Island bases. This VT-82 Avenger was part of a flight attacking Chichi Jima, 145 miles NNE of Iwo. Japanese AA disabled another TBM that collided with the one pictured, shearing off several feet of left wing. The pilot, Ens. Robert T. King, fearing his aircraft would fail, ordered his crew to bail out, then struggled for 100 miles back toward the task force. Nearing *Bennington*, he extended gear and flaps but found he had insufficient control to attempt a landing. He ditched and was rescued. (MNA)

Air and naval power were not decisive in every Pacific island contest. Months of air attacks and days of naval bombardment had achieved little against the reinforced concrete defenses of Iwo Jima.The Japanese garrison, deep in their bunkers, fought to near annihilation, extracting heavy casualties from the Marine invaders. (Author's Collection)

The Royal Navy joined Pacific operations early in 1945 and was heavily involved in Okinawa operations. HMS *Victorious*, one of five fleet carriers in the British squadron, is seen here at anchor. Her forward flight deck is filled with Vought Corsairs, and the stern shows Grumman Avengers. The ugly duckling in the center is a Supermarine Otter amphibian, much loved by air crews for its rescue capability. (Jerry Scutts)

Above: Fairey Firefly F.1s equipped 1772 Squadron of HMS *Indefatigable*. Carrying a pilot and observer, the dive bomber was equipped with four fixed 20mm cannon, two in each wing. They are seen here folding wings and being stored on the forward flight deck. (Jerry Scutts)

Below: A Supermarine Seafire, seagoing version of the Spitfire, crash lands. HMS *Indefatigable* was the only carrier of the Royal Navy's Pacific fleet equipped with this type fighter. (Jerry Scutts)

A 20 March 1945 low-level bombing attack on *Bataan* CVL-29 was unsuccessful, and the Japanese aircraft was downed by the combined fire of many ships. This is the view from *Hancock* CV-19 as the fleet delivered Ryukyu strikes. (NARS)

San Jacinto recovers her brood during Okinawa operations in March 1945. Above: An F6F of VF-45 has just landed. (USN)

Left: *Yorktown's* Air Group 9 was conducting a rocket attack on Kadena A/D on 26 March 1945 when a VF-9 Hellcat collided with the Avenger of Lt. Cdr. Byron E. Cooke, CO of VT-9. Cooke (seen here in the cockpit) and his crew were lost but the Hellcat pilot, Ens. Fred Fox, managed to get free of his aircraft. He evaded capture on Okinawa and was picked up by a mine sweeper several days later. (Leon Frankel)

A TBM-3 Avenger of VT-9 lets fly with a salvo of rockets. A broadside of 5-inch rockets was as powerful as a salvo from the combined main batteries of a destroyer. (Leon Frankel)

Above: On the hangar deck of *Essex*, F4U-1D Corsairs of VBF-83 are loaded with 5-inch rockets for a Ryukyu strike. (USN)

Below: Okinawa was invaded on 1 April 1945 after weeks of heavy air attack. Here a TBM from carrier *Hancock* 's VT-6 returns from an attack on 27 March 1945. (NARS)

Above: The British Pacific Fleet patroled southwest of Okinawa to Formosa from March to May 1945, supporting the Okinawa campaign. An 849 Squadron Avenger from carrier H.M.S. *Victorious* is seen here over Formosa. (Jerry Scutts)

Below: Lt. Cdr. David Jenkins, of 1839 Squadron, lands his F6F Hellcat on the Royal Navy carrier, *Indomitable*, after a strike on Sakashima Gunto. (NARS)

Above: Avengers of VT-6 en route to a Ryukyu Island strike. (NARS)

Below: A Stinson CV-1 Sentinel, possibly of VMO-3, jumps off the deck of carrier *Sangamon* just two days after the invasion of Okinawa. These Marine spotter aircraft lent assistance to Marine and Army artillery batteries in the ground battle. (USN)

Left: This was one of a pair of Yokosuka P1Y1 Frances bombers shot down south of Okinawa by Lt. (jg) David Sims of VC-88 on 2 April 1945. He was flying an FM-2 from *Saginaw Bay* CVE-82. (NARS)

Above: Drawing back to their mountainous defenses, the Japanese immediately ceded the mid portion of Okinawa and its two airfields to the invading force. Thus Yontan A/D was serviceable and received Marine Air Group 31 on 7 April 1945. Corsairs of VMF-311 were among the first to arrive an Yontan. It was equipped with the F4U-1C, a version armed with two 20mm cannons in each wing. (Author's Collection)

Left: A Japanese pilot of the 19th Hiko Sentai, flying from Formosa, landed on Yontan just after the invasion, unaware that the airfield had fallen to invading forces. He became a POW. (Bill Wolf)

Above: This view from a TBM shows VMF-323 Corsairs preparing for a close support rocket attack. The rugged nature of Okinawa's terrain is obvious. (USMC)

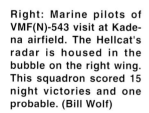

Right: Marine pilots of VMF(N)-543 visit at Kadena airfield. The Hellcat's radar is housed in the bubble on the right wing. This squadron scored 15 night victories and one probable. (Bill Wolf)

Marine Air Group 33 arrived on Okinawa's Kadena airfield on 9 April 1945. Soon thereafter, a piece of long-range Japanese artillery, aided by spotters on the high ground, zeroed in on the field and destroyed this VMF-312 Corsair. (MNA)

A checkerboard cowling F4U-1D of VMF-312 is being loaded with 500-pounders and already has eight Holy Moses rockets attached under the wings. (USMC via Bill Wolf)

5

FACING THE KAMIKAZE STORM

As the Japanese Army bitterly contested the field on Okinawa, its combined Army and Navy air forces reacted, striking the Allied invasion fleet with unbridled fury.

Even before the battle for Okinawa, a few members of the Japanese government and some ranking officers of the Imperial Navy had become convinced that the war was lost, but top Army officers derailed any move toward peace. They were bent on final costly battles, which they believed would induce Allied peace overtures. Failing that, they were prepared to commit the nation to honorable death in battle. It was with this philosophy that the military fanatics unleashed the Special Attack Corps, both volunteers and conscript pilots, organized specifically for suicide missions. Many had only minimal flight training. These tactics had first been employed with frightening results in the Philippines. The pilots were known as *Kamikaze*, Japanese for Divine Wind, after the miraculous typhoon of 1281 that destroyed a Mongol invasion fleet.

The Special Attack Units had been gathering on Kyushu, just 340 miles NNE of Okinawa, and Formosa, 300 miles WSW. Knowing that the suicide tactic could not impact the land battle, the Kamikazes were directed to maximize their destructive capability by crashing on ships of the invasion fleet. Their aircraft were an assortment of Army-Navy planes, single- and twin-engine, including obsolete trainers. Even the smallest of such aircraft, diving into a vessel, could be devastatingly destructive.

From 1 April 1945 onward, the fleet was attacked by a growing number of Japanese from both conventional squadrons and the Special Attack Units. By 6 April they were being sent in waves that guaranteed results. Combat air patrols might defeat one wave, but then have landed for fuel and ammunition before the next wave struck.

Japanese attackers focused on major warships or transports when those targets presented themselves. However, destroyers, when found, took unprecedented abuse, particularly the radar pickets, stationed alone in a position to provide early warning of impending raids. Damaged ships were also hunted, as they were often less capable of maneuvering and defending themselves from succeeding attackers.

Land-based Marine Corsair units arrived on Okinawa starting 7 April to provide close support for ground forces and were immediately forced into fighting off air attacks over the fleet. AAF fighters began arriving on 17 May 1945 and also joined in protecting the fleet, although they had been assigned the primary mission of long-range strikes in the Ryukyus and Kyushu.

Airfield space was limited as combat engineers repaired existing fields on Okinawa and created a new airdrome complex on its tiny nearby neighbor, Ie Shima. Thus, much of the Allies' enormous air strength remained in the Philippines.

Thousands of sorties were flown against the fleet in and around the Ryukyus by both conventional and Special Attack Units. These strikes tapered off by the end of May, but continued until the last days of the war. Hundreds were shot down over the Ryukyus by ships' AA or by fighters, but those that evaded the defenses extracted a toll so great that the American public was shielded from the truth by official censorship until July 1945. According to various historical records, the cost to the Allied fleet from air attacks was 57 ships sunk or damaged so severely as to be scrapped, and over 200 more damaged, with thousands of casualties among ship's crews.

On 6-7 April 1945 the Japanese launched a concentrated air attack on the Okinawa invasion fleet from Formosa and Kyushu. Over 600 aircraft took part, 355 were Kamikazes by Japanese accounts. The waves of fighters and bombers nearly overwhelmed the CAPs and managed to sink two DDs, an LST, a mine sweeper, and two cargo ships, and damaged 28 vessels including carriers, *Hancock* and *San Jacinto*. But the Japanese paid dearly for this success, with over 400 aircraft lost.

A Kamikaze hits BB *Maryland* off Okinawa on 7 April 1945. Although losing 13 killed and suffering 37 wounded, the battleship continued on station. (USN)

Navy fighters claimed 305 kills, and VF-30 from *Belleau Wood* scored a remarkable 47. Ens. Carl Foster, (center) signifies his success, a Zeke, two Tojos, and three Vals. The scene is VF-30's ready room on *Belleau Wood* on 7 April. (MNA)

Marine Air Group 31 had just arrived at Okinawa on 7 April 1945 when they were obliged to engage incoming raiders. Capt. Ralph McCormick and 1st Lt. John J. Doherty, their Corsairs seen at right, downed this Frances as seen from *Sitkoh Bay* CVE-86. (NARS)

F6F-5 Hellcats of Air Group 12 prepare to launch on the double catapults of *Randolph* CV-15 in April 1945. By this point in the war, fighter strength on all of the *Essex* class carriers had been beefed up. Air Group 12 had both fighter and fighter-bomber squadrons. VF and VBF-12 scored heavily against Japanese raiders in the Ryukyu campaign. (Author's Collection)

Left: While defending the air over the invasion fleet, Lt. (jg) David Sims destroyed a pair of Vals, one of which is seen here in his sights, on 7 April. Sims served with VC-88, *Saginaw Bay*. (NARS)

Right: On 11 April 1945 VF-23, flying CAP from *Langley,* encountered aggressive Japanese fighters over the Northern Ryukyu chain. Ens. George Bailey returned with this tail damage to his Hellcat. They lost the CO, Lt. Cdr. Merlin Paddock. VF-23 downed a pair of single-engine bombers and damaged a Tony. (MNA)

Below: 12 April, *Tennessee* BB-43, underway on the left, has just been hit by a Kamikaze that killed 23. To the right is DD *Zellars,* burning from a prior hit. (USN)

A Jill crashed just below the bridge of *Zellars* DD-777 on 12 April 1945. Destroyer *Bennion* is seen here on the left, coming alongside to offer aid. *Zellars* lost 29 killed and 37 wounded. She retired under her own power but was out of the war. (USN)

Destroyer *Sigsbee* DD-502 was on radar picket duty beyond Task Force 58 on 14 April when a single Kamikaze crashed her stern just aft the No. 5 gun turret. The explosion severed one propeller shaft and bent the other. Flooding was controled, but *Sigsbee* had to be towed to Guam, effectively putting her out of the war. She lost 22 killed and had 74 wounded. (USN)

On 16 April 1945 the Japanese dispatched dozens of bombers and Kamikazes of various types. Destroyer *Laffey* DD-724 was on radar picket duty about 50 miles NNE of Yontan when a stream of bandits began to approach her from the north. For some strange reason, *Laffey* was singled out for punishment, although there were hundreds of transports and more vulnerable targets nearby. The DD rang up its full 32 knots of speed and began to take on its attackers, first splashing four Vals. Marine Corsairs battled the oncoming stream and pursued some directly through the ship's AA. *Laffey* was subjected to 22 attacks, hit by six Kamikazes, four bombs and thoroughly strafed. She lost 31 killed and 72 wounded, yet she survived and is seen here, charred and battered. Flights from VMF-311, 322, 323 and 441 all assisted her. (NARS)

Here a Corsair of VMF-323 lugs a 160-gal. paper composition auxiliary tank. These tanks were used for Napalm by the Marines on Okinawa support missions. VMF-323 was one of the squadrons that fought off *Laffey's* attackers. (Bill Wolf)

In the second week of April the Japanese first unleashed, a manned, rocket-propelled flying bomb.

Above: The Yokosuka Model 11, had contrasting names. It was called "Oka" by the Japanese for cherry blossom, and "Baka" by the Allies, the Japanese term for foolish. Once launched it achieved over 600 mph in a dive and and packed either a 1,300 or a 2,600 lb. warhead. However, its rocket propellant permitted just a few minutes of flight, so it had to be airlifted within 50 miles of a target by slow twin-engined mother-ships that were vulnerable to attack. (NARS)

Center: Being a one-way suicide aircraft, its instruments were extremely simple, as this cockpit photo shows. (NARS)

Left: Okas had limited success against Allied ships, most being downed en route while still bonded to their transports. Here a Mitsubishi G4M Betty, with an Oka beneath, is in the sights of a Navy Hellcat. (NARS)

Above: The white nose was the trademark of VMF-322 on Okinawa. One of its pilots, 2nd Lt. Dewey Durnford is credited with what might have been the destruction of the first Betty-Baka combination. He had a total of six and one-third victories. (USMC via Bill Wolf)

Right: Ens. Alfred Lerch, was flying his F4U-1D Corsair with VF-10 northwest of Okinawa on 16 April 1945, when the squadron was vectored to many incoming bandits. The *Intrepid* CV-11 airmen claimed 33 victories, of which Lerch scored six Nates and one Val. Squadronmate, Lt. (jg) Phil Kirkwood downed four Nates and two Vals. VF-10 was the only Navy squadron to fly the Wildcat, Hellcat and Corsair in three combat tours. Despite the frantic efforts of its fighters, *Intrepid* was hit by a Kamikaze that killed ten and wounded 87, putting her out of action until August. (NARS)

On 4 May 1945, a day of deadly success for the Special Attack Corps, *Sangamon* CVE-26 was hit by two Kamikaze aircraft. Initially it appeared that the ship was a hopeless loss, as the aircraft of VC-33 fueled the fires. But the gallant crew controlled the blaze. This was the view of carnage on the flight deck the following day. *Sangamon's* losses were 46 killed and 116 wounded, and she was out of the war. Several aircraft are visible here after they burned down to their engines. (USN)

Task Force 57, the British squadron, had been assigned to interdict Japanese airfields in the Sakashima Gunto chain between Formosa and Okinawa. On 4 May 1945 a lone Zeke, evading AA and the Seafire CAP, plunged into the aft deck of carrier *Formidable.* Above: Fires rage among parked Corsairs and Avengers, eleven of which were destroyed. Note the still undamaged Corsair near the island superstructure. Crew casualties were eight killed and 50 wounded. (Jerry Scutts) Below: The steel flight deck, common to Royal Navy carriers, helped to limit *Formidable's* damage below decks. Her crew was able to clear this incredible mass of wreckage and commence flight operations within six hours. *Formidable* suffered another Kamikaze crash on her aft flight deck on 9 May with only one killed and seven aircraft destroyed, but this time she was forced to retire. (Jerry Scutts)

Left: Mid-morning on 11 May 1945 a Zeke dove out of low clouds to crash the deck of the *Bunker Hill* CV-17. Minutes later a Judy also dove on the carrier. The results of the two strikes was the raging inferno seen here. The fires were eventually controlled and *Bunker Hill* retired to the West Coast for repairs. But she lost 396 personnel and had 264 wounded. (NARS)

Below: VF-9 served on four aircraft carriers during three tours of combat. Its final home was *Yorktown* CV-10 from March to June 1945. This foursome from VF-9 was the highest scoring division in the USN during WW II. (L. to R.) Lt. (jg) Harris Mitchell, 10 victories; Lt (jg) Clinton Smith, six victories; Lt. (jg) James French, 11 victories; and Lt. Gene Valencia, who served two tours of combat, 23 victories. They tallied their final kills fighting Japanese raiders north of Okinawa on 11 May 1945. (Barrett Tillman)

Another Japanese operation, borne of desperation to aid their Okinawa Army, was launched the night of 24 May 1945. Several Sally bombers of the 3rd Dikotori Hikotai, each loaded with ten elite infantrymen and three air crew members, departed Kyushu for Okinawa, determined to land on Yontan and Kadena for a commando attack. Several turned back, and five were downed by AA fire. One (shown above) managed to crash land on Yontan. Its team, carrying demolition charges, destroyed nine aircraft, (below are burned Douglas R5D transports), damaged another 29, fired a fuel dump and caused one death and 18 other casualties before being annihilated. (NARS)

6

DEATH SORTIE

As Okinawa was invaded the Imperial Navy high command set in motion a response that had all the elements of a Wagnerian tragedy. It was conceived in an atmosphere of fanatical fatalism, with the Emperor's imprimatur. Mighty battleship *Yamato*, with seven escorts, was dispatched from Japan in the implausible hope that they might attack the thin-skinned invasion transports in Kerama Retto anchorage thereby supporting the Japanese Army on Okinawa. Other major units of the Japanese Navy still afloat were too damaged to join.

It was planned as a one-way mission, since *Yamato* did not carry sufficient fuel for the return to Japan. Her meager escort included light cruiser *Yahagi* and eight destroyers. Soon after departing the Inland Sea they were sighted by a U.S. submarine. Despite a devious approach by the Japanese force, submarines continued to shadow until long-range Navy patrol aircraft took up the watch, dashing any hope of surprise.

Yamato had no air protection, and the Japanese knew the consequences of such folly. Early in the war they had shocked the Royal Navy by an air assault on battleships, *Prince of Wales* and *Repulse*, sinking these dreadnoughts that had sailed from Singapore lacking air cover.

On 7 April 1945, 200 miles north of Okinawa in the East China Sea, aircraft from Task Force 58 "cornered" the *Yamato* squadron and began attacking in waves with torpedoes, bombs, rockets, and machine guns. 170 aircraft from 13 carriers participated, flying through extremely heavy flak. *Yamato* alone mounted over 100 AA guns, and fired her main 18 inch batteries in the water ahead of torpedo bombers, raising deadly plumes of water. The outcome, however, was inevitable.

After a two-hour running battle, *Yamato*, *Yahagi*, and six of the eight destroyers were sunk with a loss of over 3,400 crew members. U.S. Navy losses were ten aircraft and a dozen men.

The 70,000-ton battleship *Yamato* (center) and her escorts are seen from several miles away by a shadowing Martin PBM-5 Mariner of VPB-21. (Don Sweet)

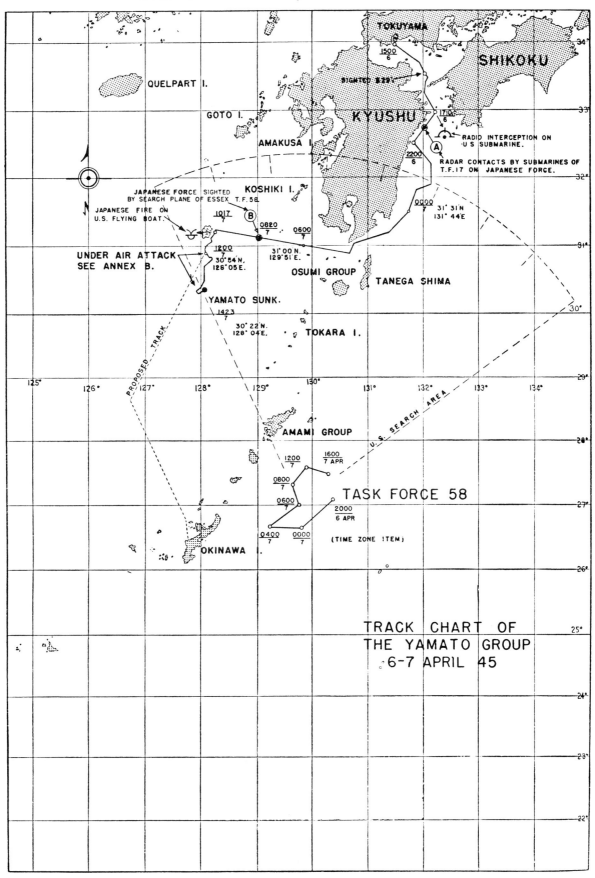

Source: U.S. Strategic Bombing Survey, 1946, The Campaigns of the Pacific War, Appendix 100.

A pair of PBM-5 flying boats from VPB-21 shadowed the Japanese ships for five hours and homed in the strikes that were dispatched from Task Force 58.

Above: A VPB-21 Mariner in flight. (Richard L. Simms)

Below: One of the VPB-21 Mariners at anchor off Okinawa. (Fred Dickey via Don Sweet)

For the attack on *Yamato*, Task Force 58 air groups loaded special ordnance not often utilized in the later stages of the war.

Above: *Wasp* crewmen ready a 1,000 lb. armor-piercing bomb for a VB-86 Helldiver. (USN)

Below: A 2,000 lb. torpedo is backed under the bomb bay of a VT-45 Avenger aboard *San Jacinto*. This was to be the last U.S. Navy torpedo attack of World War II. (USN)

Above: A VF-82 Hellcat prepares to launch from *Bennington*, whose Air Group 82 claims to have made the first hits on *Yamato*. (USN)

Below: Plowing through the East China Sea at flank speed, the great warship *Yamato* unleashes a torrent of AA fire from her 100-plus flak batteries as it maneuvers to avoid attack. She smokes aft from prior hits as a bomb creates a plume of water on her port side.(MNA)

Above: Light Cruiser *Yahagi* is seen, already dead in the water and leaking fuel, as more bombs burst around her. She ultimately sank after twelve bomb and seven torpedo hits. (MNA)

Right: The *Yamato* task force downed ten Navy aircraft and damaged many more. A Curtiss SB2C-4 from VB-9 had its wing peeled open but returned to *Yorktown.* (Leon Frankel)

These airmen are typical of the young U.S. Naval aviators who attacked the *Yamato* squadron.

Left: Lt. Cdr. Tony Schneider, CO of VB-9. (Leon Frankel)

Right: Lt. (jg) Leon Frankel, age 21, of VT-9. (Leon Frankel)

Left: The TBM-3 of Lt. (jg) W. E. Delaney, of *Belleau Wood's* VT-30, was a victim of Japanese AA fire. He and his crew parachuted. The two enlisted men were lost, but Delaney managed to inflate his life raft. While a VPB-21 Mariner piloted by Lt. (jg) Richard Simms distracted Japanese gunners and drew their fire, the PBM of Lt. James Young landed and rescued Delaney. (R.L. Simms)

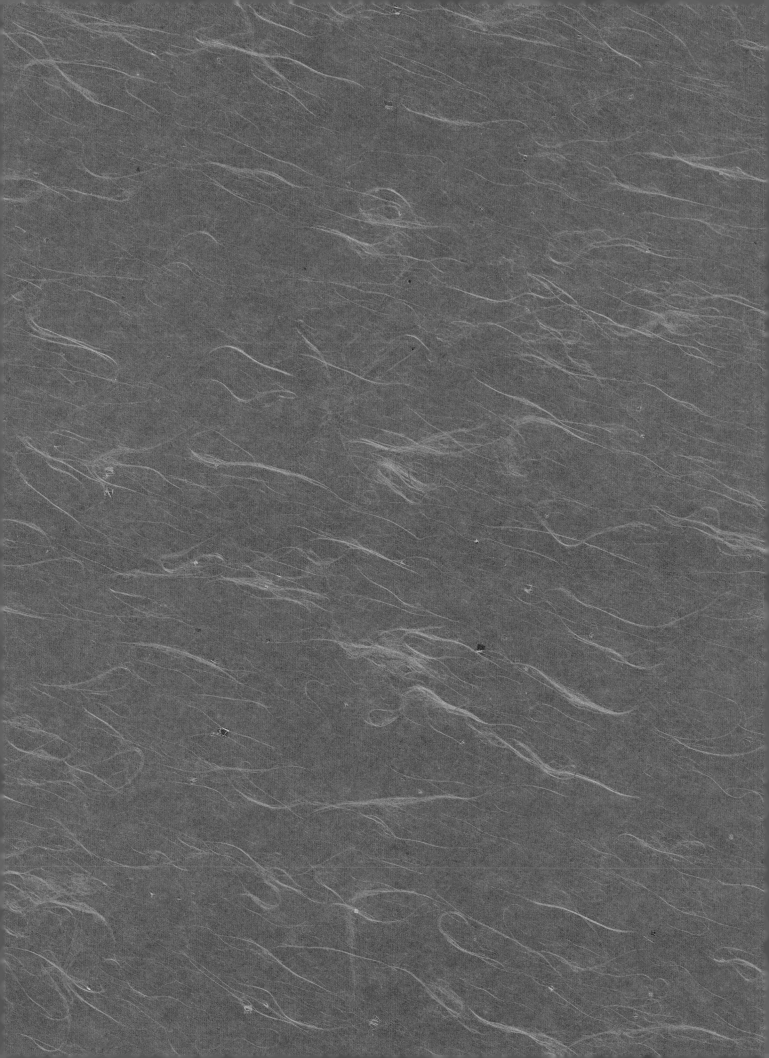